Cooking
SCHOOL

Middle Eastern Food

SARA GILBERT

CREATIVE EDUCATION & CREATIVE PAPERBACKS

Published by Creative Education and Creative Paperbacks
P.O. Box 227, Mankato, Minnesota 56002 • Creative Education and
Creative Paperbacks are imprints of The Creative Company
www.thecreativecompany.us

Design and production by Christine Vanderbeek
Printed in the United States of America

Photographs by Alamy (Funky Stock–Paul Williams, Photocuisine),
Corbis (Image Source; Leatart, Brian/the food passionates), Dreamstime
(Lena Andersson),Getty Images (Photostock Israel, Howard Shooter),
iStockphoto (naelnabil), Shutterstock (alisafarov, ANCH, area381, Art
Allianz, bonchan, Vitaly Korovin, mehmetcan, NEGOVURA, KIM
NGUYEN, Ildi Papp, pogonici, Elena M. Tarasova, Evlakhov Valeriy,
VolkOFF-ZS-BP, Yganko), SuperStock (F1 ONLINE, Radius)

Library of Congress Cataloging-in-Publication Data
Gilbert, Sara. • Middle Eastern food / by Sara Gilbert. • p. cm. —
(Cooking school) • Summary: An elementary introduction to the
relationship between cooking and Middle Eastern food, the
effect of local agriculture on the diets of different regions,
common tools such as pestles, and recipe instructions.
Includes bibliographical references
and index. • ISBN 978-1-60818-
505-4 (hardcover) • ISBN 978-
1-62832-099-2 (pbk)
1. Cooking, Middle Eastern—
Juvenile literature. 2. Food—
Middle East—Juvenile literature.
I. Title. • TX725.M628G55 2015
641.59'56—dc23   2014002300

CCSS: RI.1.1, 2, 3, 5, 6, 7; RI.2.1, 2,
3, 5, 6, 7; RI.3.1, 3, 5, 7; RF.1.1;
RF.2.3, 4; RF.3.3

First Edition
9 8 7 6 5 4 3 2 1

Table of Contents

Delicious Foods

People all around the world cook food. They cook because they need to eat. They cook because it's fun to make tasty, *nutritious* food. Cooks in the Middle East are known for making healthy meals with fruits and vegetables.

People in the Middle East often eat using only their right hand.

Healthy Cooking

Long ago, Asian, African, and European *traders* enjoyed the olives, spices, and vegetables in the Middle East. Middle Eastern cooking still uses those healthy *ingredients*.

Middle Eastern street markets sell mounds of herbs and spices.

Taste of the Middle East

In northern Africa, couscous is part of many meals. It can be made with fresh vegetables, served in a *stew*, or sprinkled with cinnamon and sugar for dessert.

People add spices and toppings to make colorful couscous dishes.

People in Turkey cook with seafood. Around the Black Sea, people eat tiny fish called anchovies.

People grill large fish (left). They bake anchovies with rice.

Kebabs come from the Middle Eastern country of Iran. A lamb kebab is usually cooked over an open flame and served with rice.

Legend says that soldiers cooked the first kebabs with swords.

Lebanese meals often include several small bowls filled with spreads and dips like hummus. Beans called chickpeas (pictured) are mashed to make hummus.

"Meze" is the name for small dishes eaten before the main meal.

Grinding Spices

Many Middle Eastern cooks grind spices and crush garlic. They use a flat tool called a pestle with a heavy bowl called a mortar to do this.

A mortar and pestle are used to grind peppers into powder.

Hummus

is usually eaten with pita chips or bread.

INGREDIENTS

1 can chickpeas

2 tablespoons minced garlic

¼ cup lemon juice

¼ cup olive oil

salt and pepper

water

pita bread, carrot sticks, or cucumber slices for serving

DIRECTIONS

1. Drain the liquid from a can of chickpeas.

2. Combine chickpeas, 2 tablespoons minced garlic, ¼ cup lemon juice, ¼ cup olive oil, and salt and pepper in a blender.

3. Add a little water, and blend until smooth.

4. Serve your hummus in a bowl with pita bread, carrot sticks, or cucumber slices.

Couscous

is a grain that can be mixed with many things.

INGREDIENTS

2 cups water

1 cup instant couscous

1 teaspoon salt

1 tablespoon olive oil

vegetables or cinnamon and sugar

DIRECTIONS

1. Boil 2 cups water in a small pot. Then turn off the heat.

2. Put 1 cup instant couscous, 1 teaspoon salt, and 1 tablespoon olive oil in a shallow baking dish. Pour the hot water over it. Cover the dish and let sit for 15 minutes.

3. Remove the cover, and fluff the couscous with a fork. Add vegetables, or sprinkle with cinnamon and sugar, then enjoy!

Middle Eastern kebabs

are made with lamb, but you can use
other meats or just vegetables, too.

INGREDIENTS

cubes of meat

onions

grape tomatoes

peppers

DIRECTIONS

1. Soak wooden skewers in water for at least an hour.

2. Carefully place cubes of meat and vegetables on each skewer.

3. Have an adult grill the kebabs. Then slide the cubes off the skewer and eat!

Glossary

ingredients any of the foods or liquids that combine to complete a recipe

nutritious healthy and good for you

stew a dish of meat and vegetables cooked slowly in liquid

traders people who travel to buy or sell foods, fabrics, or other products

Read More

Blaxland, Wendy. *I Can Cook! Middle Eastern Food.* Mankato, Minn.: Smart Apple Media, 2011.

Crocker, Betty. *Betty Crocker Kids Cook!* Minneapolis: Betty Crocker, 2007.

Low, Jennifer. *Kitchen for Kids.* New York: Whitecap Books, 2010.

Websites

http://www.pbs.org/food/theme/cooking -with-kids/
Find easy recipes to try by yourself or with an adult's assistance.

http://www.foodnetwork.com/cooking -with-kids/package/index.html
Learn to cook with celebrity chefs on the website of television's Food Network.

Note: Every effort has been made to ensure that the websites listed above are suitable for children, that they have educational value, and that they contain no inappropriate material. However, because of the nature of the Internet, it is impossible to guarantee that these sites will remain active indefinitely or that their contents will not be altered.

Index